Cleopatra

The True and Surprising Story of the Queen of the Nile

Table of Contents

Introduction:
Why History Matters

I want to thank you and congratulate you for downloading the book, *"Cleopatra"*.

This book contains useful information about one of the most famous queens in history. It was not uncommon for the ancient Egyptians to view woman as equal to men, and allow them to enjoy power, but Cleopatra was the sole ruler of the throne which makes her unique. There is much to be learned by looking to events and rulers of the past.

History is a fascinating subject, but not everyone understands why it is relevant or necessary to research. What is point of studying ancient people and events? How can these things possibly matter to us modern humans, when they happened hundreds or even thousands of years ago? Yes, Cleopatra was an influential woman in her time, but what does that have to do with us now?

These persistent and ever-present questions about why history is relevant to us in today's world could be the result of which forces shaped our history as citizens of the United States. Our nation's story is presented to us as a proud tale of bravery, where the discoverer of the country forged America using means that appear questionable to some. For this reason, our connection to history is different. It is much shorter than the history of other nations, which has separated us, in a sense, from typical demands of history on our cultural and social identity.

Remembering Our Roots to Gain Wisdom

The result of this lack of traditional demands has led to a lot of questioning as to whether our history is even true. Much of that skepticism is normal and healthy, but remembering roots is important. The current scholarly obsession with only focusing on the present or recent events and ignoring ancient history is severely limiting.

This focus on the present appears to have intensified especially within the last couple of decades with the rises in digital technology and prevalence. The new rules set before us pertaining to this digital age make looking to the ancient past even more unnecessary, but we may be missing something very important if we forgo that ability. This brings us again to the question- why should we study cultures of ancient history? Is there something we can learn from looking to ancient Mesopotamia, where Eden is rumored to have existed? This area has been called the cradle that civilization sprung from, possessing early versions of complex and organized social systems and the (at the time) new advent of writing. In addition to the social structures and the use of writing, a lot of valuable art has come from this ancient land.

How Ancient Art, People and Practices affect us Today

Do these ancient practices and, art, literature and events have anything to do with our modern world? Some say they do, and that we owe everything to those ancient humans and the way they interacted with the world, the things they created and even the myths they crafted and passed down as a way to explain their surroundings. Study of the ancient world and its rulers has more than just academic benefits to be gained from it. Not only can we become wiser to facts about our history by undertaking these studies, but we can also uncover knowledge about what it means to be human, how social dynamics work and how we as people have interacted with each other in the past.

To study the past means to be encouraged to look deeper and figure out what defined cultures of the old world, and how they relate to our world today. This means that getting in touch with the past is necessary for truly knowing ourselves, and others, in the present day. Without this knowledge of how humans developed and where they sprang from and the steps our ancestors took to get the world to where it is in the present, we can never fully understand the reasons behind why we act or think how we do. Without this knowledge, we will also be ill-equipped to make constructive decisions about the best ways to advance and change as societies, people and nations.

Why do we Still Talk about Cleopatra?

If you mention the name Cleopatra, people probably think of Elizabeth Taylor or maybe the love story that transpired between her and Julius Caesar, or her and Mark Antony. Others may first think of her, what was rumored to be, exceptional beauty. It turns out, however, that there is a lot more to her than this and that we have underestimated this historical figure greatly.

This book will attempt to contribute to our understanding and appreciation by looking to the life of this extremely influential and important woman in history. We will look at specific characteristics of her life, decisions she made and the events that transpired during her reign, so that we can better understand ourselves and the world we live in.

Women in the days of ancient Egypt had rights that would not come about again for women in general for centuries. They practiced medicine, were in charge of vineyards and even owned their own ships. These freedoms may have been the result of the importance of certain gods, such as Isis, the powerful female god. This reverence for female power may have contributed to the existence of strong queen figures in the old times of Egypt. Although Cleopatra was not the first powerful female in those times, she was the first one to rule the throne all by herself which makes her stand out and remain remembered all these years later.

Thanks again for downloading this book, I hope you enjoy it!

information is without contract or any type of guarantee assurance.

The trademarks that are used are without any consent, and the publication of the trademark is without permission or backing by the trademark owner. All trademarks and brands within this book are for clarifying purposes only and are the owned by the owners themselves, not affiliated with this document.

Chapter 1:
The Earliest Known Days of Cleopatra

Cleopatra was the last ruler and queen of the dynasty of Macedonia. The line of rule she sprang from had been around since 323 B.C. when Alexander the Great passed, and would continue on unmatched in power until 30 B.C. when Rome prevailed. A woman of legend, her name will not soon be forgotten even though thousands of years have passed.

Cleopatra's Parents

This historical figure's family ruled over ancient Egypt for over a century before Cleopatra VII Thea Philopator was born in 69 B.C. The threat of the Romans would dominate her life exactly as it had dominated the life of her father. Cleopatra was no stranger to hardship, and instead of letting this intimidate her or make her weak she turned it to her distinct advantage and became a legend. She was the second born of five siblings, her father being Ptolemy XII Neos Dionysos who had been in power over Egypt since Ptolemy X Alexander II passed in 80 B.C.

Although no one knows for sure who Cleopatra's mother was, historians have surmised as to her identity and the likelihood that she was King Ptolemy XII's sister, Cleopatra V Tryphena. There have also been suggestions that Cleopatra's mother was King Ptolemy XII's half-sister or cousin, though we can never know for sure. The reason this is suspected is that there is lot of evidence that points to her mother being of Egyptian descent and quite possibly related to a high priest at the Ptah temple, the creator god who gave her father the crown and who was considered the most important of all priests during that time.

Ptolemy XII's Death and what it meant for Cleopatra

In 51 B.C. Cleopatra's father, Ptolemy XII, passed away and left the throne to his 18 year old daughter and her younger sibling, 10 year old Ptolemy XIII. Much is unknown about her early years, similar to the mystery of who her mother was. We do know that she seemed to appear suddenly on the scene of history some time near 50 B.C. and become a successful young queen, fully capable of rivaling her competitors.

She was more than able to keep up with the Romans and engage their interest - including the interest of Julius Caesar - but how she came to be such a capable leader is largely a mystery to us due to the blank spot in history concerning her formative childhood and teenage years. What can be known for sure is that she possessed a remarkable level of intelligence and cunning, or she never would have made it as far as she did.

There have also been extensive debates throughout history about the ethnicity of Cleopatra VII. While many believed for centuries that she was Greek, others suspect that she may have been of black African descent. Regardless of the race she was, her power was unmistakable and women and men of all races can be inspired by her. It has been said that the young queen married her brother, since that was not uncommon during those times. In the following years their home country of Egypt went through a number of struggles including economic issues, floods and widespread famine.

Cleopatra's Mysterious Upbringing 69 – B.C.

Legends state that Cleopatra was such a success because of her sexuality and physical appeal, but other sources point to her charm and intelligence as being responsible for her legacy. While many stories focus on her exceptional physical beauty, others claim that she was average looking. This remarkable woman was rumored to speak, or at least be able to understand, up to eight different languages. She was also reported to be the first royal in the entire dynasty to learn the language of Egyptian, which is what her subjects spoke. It is also supposed that she was an author who wrote extensively on subjects including cosmetics, measures and weights and possibly even magic.

From this, we can surmise that although we don't know the details of her upbringing, her formative years included a quality education. Not only does her knowledge of languages and writing skills point to this, but her successful strategizing later on in her ruling proves that she was no stranger to academics and critical thinking and must have had more great tutors than historians are even aware of from a young age.

In the second and third centuries of ancient Egypt, famous scholars and poets were often the tutors of princesses and princes in the Ptolemaic system. Historians assume that Cleopatra and her brother were no exception, since she educated her own kids in that fashion. Nikolaos of Damascus, the famous philosopher and historian, was the tutor she hired for the twin children she had with her husband, Mark Antony, in 40 B.C.

Though it can be assumed she had notable tutors that contributed to her education, the most influential teacher of her time was most likely Ptolemy XII- her own father.

Intellectual training is all well and good for shaping a young mind, but where Cleopatra gained a true advantage was from being able to directly observe and learn from the experiences of her dad.

Chapter 2:
Her Father and how his Ruling Affected Her

Cleopatra's father was obsessed with retaining his throne by any means necessary. Ptolemy XII had an intense interest in Dionysos, the Greek god of music and wine, whom the people of Greece related to Osiris who was the Egyptian royal deity. In addition to his interests in playing Dionysiac music on his flute he had passionate religious views, some of which drew criticism from historians in later years.

Ptolemy XII's Influence on her Later Strategies

Though his young daughter likely didn't understand very much of her father's religious views and the theology at the foundation of them, she was observant of the effects of this on his court. It possessed qualities of musical inspiration and sensuality and is thought to have contributed to her intelligent uses of spectacles of religion to advance her political career later on in life. To be a successful leader one must be able to relate to all types of people, and this was a skill Cleopatra learned early on and benefited from throughout her years of life.

The most important contributions Ptolemy XII made to his daughter's education, however, were through his own struggles concerning politics in a practical sense. She watched him learn harsh lessons about fighting to maintain his position of power in the face of constant competition both from his own family members and from ambitious politicians of Rome.

Ptolemy XII had a grip on his throne, but there were constant threats to this from the very moment he seized it in 80 B.C. The man was an illegitimate son to his father, Ptolemy IX, and he was constantly being challenged and having his ruling rights questioned. Among those who questioned him were politicians of Rome who saw Egypt as a valuable prize to be stolen and even made claims that the last legitimate king of Egypt, Ptolemy X Alexander II, had signed his empire to Rome in the case that he died without an heir.

The dangers the will of Ptolemy X posed become apparent in the year 63 B.C., when young Cleopatra was only seven. A man named P. Servilius Rullus, a tribune of Rome, suggested that the people of Rome annex the great nation of Egypt as was requested in Ptolemy X's will. He then suggested that they take over the rich farming land of Egypt to support a scheme that he claimed was intended to give land to the needy people of Rome.

Given this man's track record, it was hard to know whether he was being truthful about his pure intentions to help the poor of Rome and people were skeptical of what he truly intended to do with the land. This could have seriously altered the structure of the city and been dangerous.

Luckily for Ptolemy XII, however, the Roman tribune Rullus' attempts to pass this legislation were not successful. Politics in Rome in the mid and later parts of the 60s B.C. were largely controlled by the Romans' fearing Pompey. Pompey had recently defeated Mithridates VI of Pontus and was working on creating a prestigious reputation for himself, along with a loyal following, as he ran a successful campaign in the Near East region.

Rullus made claims about intending to help the Roman citizens, but his true motivation in the schemes he suggested were helping Pompey. He would have done this by giving him an efficient military command for the rivals of Pompey; Gaius Julius Caesar and Marcus Licinius Crassus. His attempts at gaining property were mostly for selfish reasons, or to support the questionable tyrant who would eventually be overthrown and taken over.

Ptolemy XII's Will and Determination to have his Children Inherit his Throne

The long and varied reign of Ptolemy XII ended similarly to how it started; fraught with fears and concerns about who would succeed the throne. He had his children deified and appointed Cleopatra to rule alongside him, which clearly highlighted the fact that he wished for his children to be his successors. However these actions did not help to get rid of the danger that Rome was posing against Egypt, which was gaining even more traction due to the large debts Ptolemy XII had accumulated during his attempts to maintain his throne.

Similarly to the ruler who preceded him, Ptolemy X, he crafted a will that favored the people of Rome- not naming them as heirs but as the mass guardians of his daughter Cleopatra and his oldest son Ptolemy XIII. The two siblings were to be married and take over his throne as siblings and partners, ruling Egypt together.

As soon as he deposited a single copy of the written will in the city of Alexandria for safety purposes and sent the second to Pompey, who was given the task of presenting it at the Senate, the ruler Ptolemy XII passed away in the year 51 B.C. during the springtime. He had done everything possible to ensure the survival of his ruling bloodline and dynasty, and once that had been completed it was time to go.

Chapter 3:
How Cleopatra Seized the Throne

Ptolemy XII had the intention that his children would rule together, the way that Cleopatra and he had. However, this was not very likely to happen. Cleopatra, though still quite young at the time, was nearly 10 years older than her brother and her observations of her father and general life in the 50s B.C. had gotten her ready to face a powerful position.

Her younger brother Ptolemy XIII was still a child, and only had life experiences of events that had taken place in the Alexandria palace he lived in, whereas Cleopatra had already seen a lot and gained knowledge during her teen years from watching her father struggle politically and strategize about ruling. She saw him face challenges and overcome them, as well as determinedly maintaining his throne in the face of constant threat. An observant and intelligent girl, she had learned much from this and was fit to rule even at her young age.

Learning from her Father's Mistakes and Successes

Cleopatra had been present for the humiliating attempts the Romans had made to overthrow or manipulate her father and had observed his suffering. The young woman had also seen Ptolemy XII's brilliant return to the throne in the year 54 B.C., and the revenge he had enacted out of fear toward her sister and those who supported her. Perhaps it is not so surprising that young Cleopatra didn't take long to reveal that she had no intention of sharing her throne. Instead of giving in to her brother's supremacy as was the intention of her father, she would carry out different plans- rejecting the plans the court faction and Pothinos the eunuch had for her.

Not long after her father's passing, Cleopatra made sure to assert her claim to sole ownership of the throne. She adopted the name Thea Philopatora (which translates to "Goddess who loves her father"), which was cleverly selected to make it sound as though he had wished for her to be the real successor of his throne. In addition to this, Cleopatra had worked hard to garner support for her sole ownership of the throne in the upper area of the country where her dad had a strong support system. For nearly 200 years, Upper Egypt (Thebaid in particular) had been a large source of unrest in Egypt.

Starting around 80 B.C., Ptolemy X had taken great lengths to suppress a rebellion of the natives near there, ruining a large portion of Thebes with his brutal methods. Similar to many of the pharaohs that came before him, Ptolemy XII had sought out support in that area by supporting and aiding extravagant building of temples in the sanctuary areas. He knew that this would be a beneficial move, and his intuition was not mistaken.

He also made sure to cultivate the noble and priestly family sectors in the area, who considered government offices and temple structures as family heirlooms of great importance. He was careful in his strategizing and built support through careful means that took time and effort, and Cleopatra saw her opportunity to use his efforts to her advantage. There was never a moment that she was not looking for strategic moves to improve her chances at achieving goals, which is one of the factors that made her such a fantastic and effective leader.

Cleopatra's Early Strategizing and Garnering of Support of Upper Egypt

In 52 B.C., the elderly Buchis bull died and priests of Egypt discovered a new bull to take its place. The resourceful and new ruler saw a great chance with this event and seized this opportunity to continue her father's successful and popular policies in the upper region of Egypt. Both Romans and Greeks alike were typically fascinated by the Egyptian ways of religion, but their puzzlement and shock in response to cults of animals that were considered sacred was unmatched. Nearly every god was believed by Egyptian religion to have the potential to appear in specific animals.

Near the closing of the first millennium B.C., the Egyptians' reverence for holy animals had reached the point of centrality for popular cults in the area and people's devotion often took quite extreme modes of expression. Diodoros, the ancient historian who was reported to have visited Egypt in 60 B.C., watched a Roman embassy member get ripped apart by an angry group of mobbing people because he had killed a feline by accident.

A sacred and holy spot in the religion of Egyptians, however, was taken up by a select few animals who people claimed were the reincarnated versions of certain deities. These animals were recognizable by specific markings and, for this reason, stood out to people. When one of these animals died, a successor would be sought out and discovered and a period of great celebrations would follow the joyous event. These animals were treated as royal, pharaoh-like beings during their lives, and once they died they were given special burial treatment. These sacred animals were mummified and decadently buried in catacombs underground, as if they were kings.

How the Buchis Bull Helped Cleopatra Win Loyalty

The Buchis bull mentioned earlier was one such "reincarnated" animal, and exceptionally famous when compared to others. This bull could be recognized by his white body, black colored face and the direction his hair growth took (backwards). People everywhere claimed that this holy bull could change his colors as often as every hour, at will. The Egyptians believed that Buchis the bull was the reincarnated soul of the solar god Montu of Hermonthis, which was a city close to Thebes. Cleopatra, the young and ambitious new ruler, took the chance she saw with the installation of the second version of Buchis the bull in 51 B.C. This was her chance to take over and benefit from the loyalty of those who supported her father in Upper Egypt.

Her attempts were a great success, and years later as her conqueror (Augustus the emperor of Rome) reigned, everyone would recall how the goddess who loves her father, the Lady of the Two Lands, rowed Buchis the bull in an Amun barque, joining with the king's boats and all of the citizens of the city of Thebes. The priests and Hermonthis were with him, which made the event all the more special to the inhabitants of the city with their great reverence for incarnated deities in animal form.

It is unclear whether Cleopatra herself held the same beliefs as these citizens, or whether this was only a clever tactic to gain support from Upper Egypt. Either way, it was a strategic and successful move that would benefit her later on and showed great promise of her capabilities as a ruler. It was smart moves like this that shaped her as a fearless and impacting leader who would be remembered for all time. There would be many more intelligent choices like this later on in her days of ruling.

Cleopatra's Interactions and Intentions with Thebaid

This remarkable woman was also able to secure support from the aristocracy of Upper Egypt, which included Kallimakhos the governor of the Thebaid. This was an impressive feat, as this man was considered essentially a viceroy who ruled the upper part of Egypt. Cleopatra was ambitious and determined in her ventures into Upper Egypt and because of this was wildly successful. She was so successful in this venture that the Thebaid offered to support her through the conquest of Egypt from Octavian in 30 B.C. and remained loyal to her throughout her entire, substantial reign.

Although this was a significant gain for Cleopatra and benefited her a lot, the main political power of Egypt in the Ptolemaic era did not lie in the Thebaid. It lay instead in Alexandria, the capital city, whose active and assertive body of citizens had seen the rise and fall of countless kings over the century. Cleopatra, unfortunately, only had a few loyal supports in Alexandria- much to her disappointment.

The Greeks of Alexandria had seen Ptolemy XII as their first selection for the ruling king in the year 80 B.C., but regardless of this support his relations with them had taken on a bitter edge throughout the course of his time of rule. For this reason, his daughter and successor was the new target for their hostility and frustrations. Perhaps even worse than this for the citizens, the specific ambitions that Cleopatra held were in direct contradiction to her dynasty's closely held traditional values. Queens of the Ptolemaic era, including Cleopatra I and Arsinoe II, had held a substantial amount of influence in this era but this was just as the regent or consort of the rule of a king. What this meant was that Ptolemy XIII, Cleopatra's brother, received the support of loyalists to the Ptolemaic rule, instead of the ambitious ruler herself.

Among these Ptolemaic loyalists were a sector known as the Gabinians, who were largely responsible for keeping Cleopatra's father on his throne in the later years of his rule. Once he had died though, Cleopatra further frustrated and alienated these people by choosing to hand over multiple Gainians to Syria's governor to take responsibility for the murder of two of an important Roman politician's sons.

The First Hints of Cleopatra's Historical Success and Fame

Historical accounts of this time period only give a glimpse into the outline of Cleopatra's early struggles to gain power, in a very general way. It appears that in the early days her audacity and speed contributed largely to the success she would enjoy in the later years of her life. For the end of 51 B.C. and first portion of the year 50 B.C., her rise to power is made clear by the fact that Ptolemy XIII's name virtually started disappearing from all documents from that time period. Official papers stated nothing of him, which suggests that her power was unmatchable to her younger sibling and that she soon became the focus of the ruling throne.

As the era of 50 B.C. fell however, the new ruler's ambitious attempts at securing lone power of the throne were not very successful. Disastrous famines struck the nation of Egypt and caused a tragically low level of the Nile. This gave those who wished to defeat her the perfect chance to make their attempt. Enemies took this chance enthusiastically and were able to undermine her successful support in the upper part of Egypt, as well as get stronger and more loyal support from citizens of the capital city Alexandria.

There was an official decree passed in the fall of the year 50 B.C. under the names Cleopatra and Ptolemy XIII that gave orders to merchants to hand over grains gathered in Upper Egypt to the capital city, and even stated that violators of this new law would be sentenced to death.

Cleopatra was understandably desperate at this point, and it's been surmised that she attempted to secure a more easily compliant spouse in her brother Ptolemy XIV, who was essentially meant to replace Ptolemy XIII. This plan appears to have been foiled when she was made to escape from the capital city of Alexandra during the year 49 B.C. Cleopatra first took refuge near the Thebaid and eventually traveled to both southern Syria and Palestine, seeking out support from friends of her passed father.

The Faceoff at the Border and what it meant for Cleopatra

From here she went on to collect a decent, if small, army and returned to try to invade her home nation of Egypt. This ambitious advance only lasted a short while and she was caught at the border by forces of her royal sibling, Ptolemy XIII. These forces were in possession of one important fortress, the key of Pelusium, which allowed them to close off the road along the coast into Egypt from Sinai.

At this point she was probably getting even more desperate, and knew that her final demise was not only possible but likely. Perhaps it is quite ironic that she was then rescued by the unforeseen reappearance of Roman influence in the affairs of her home country Egypt.

It was true that the great nation of Egypt survived, but the amazing kingdom that had been inherited by Cleopatra was not as strong as it once was. It had been robbed of its possessions, gone through intense economic hardship and been inflicted with nearly constant strife in a dynastic sense. Regardless of those factors Egypt remained attractive to politicians of Rome, who saw it as a prize to be won. Starting from the day Cleopatra received the throne in 50 B.C., she fought to reverse the decline of the nation and had some major successes.

But even though the country's chances of improving appeared bleak and brightened as she reigned, the ruler was smart enough to see that staying independent from Rome was just not realistic or beneficial. She made sure Egypt was secure by making it absolutely necessary for Roman plans to be successful in the east of the Mediterranean. This was a large motivating force behind much of her efforts and strategies during her reign.

Chapter 4:
Cleopatra and Julius Caesar

Plutarch records state that before Caesar had ever set foot in Theodotus at Egypt, Ptolemy XIII's tutor had ventured out to sea to meet him bringing along Pompey's severed head. This gesture was meant to gain favor with Julius Caesar and encourage him to head to Rome right away, since his business in Egypt could effectively be finished. The gesture, however, had quite the opposite effect that the tutor had hoped for. Julius Caesar was extremely angry about the murder of Pompey (who was his son in law), and saw it as cowardly and unnecessary.

There is a possibility that the intention of Caesar was to show Pompey mercy (which was customary in his interactions with enemies), since he openly wept when he saw the head and then immediately took steps to preserve it until it could be buried properly.

Another source hints at the possibility that Julius was planning to murder Pompey but was disappointed in the fashion in which it occurred- under a foreigner's orders- and perhaps his open weeping was exaggerated for politically beneficial reasons. Regardless of his exact reaction, it is sure that this event contributed to his ill feelings for Ptolemy XIII.

Not long after this, Pothinus, who guarded Ptolemy XIII and is said to have been the strongest force behind the throne, successfully enraged a mob in Alexandria against Julius Caesar but Caesar did not get intimidated easily. Instead Julius landed with a force that was small but powerful and headed up to the palace. Caesar then commanded that Cleopatra and Ptolemy were to release their armies and took it upon himself to remind Pothinus that Ptolemy Auletes' heirs had a debt of 6000 talents to him (a substantial amount of money.)

The Legendary Meeting of Cleopatra and Caesar

Pothinus did not appreciate this defiance to his orders (since he was the chancellor of Egypt, he controlled the nation's finances at the time) and did not bother to hide his insolent feelings towards Caesar, which ended up having devastating consequences for the man he was supposed to have been guarding- Ptolemy. Cleopatra, again always seeking opportunity and advantage, saw a chance to benefit. She was determined to seize the opportunity of Pothinus' mistake and even arranged a meeting in secret with Julius Caesar. Plutarch reveals a legendary story that states that the brave woman hid in a carpet roll until she could reveal herself to Caesar, and then presented herself in a veil.

It may have been her beauty, or her prestigious lineage (she was descended from Alexander the Great). It may have been her charisma or courage that charmed Julius, but from this point on the two became lovers. Julius reversed his decision right away about Pompey, and instead gave power back to Cleoopatra and her brother. Whatever it was that she did to win him over and gain his trust and admiration, it undoubtedly worked well.

When her brother showed up to meet with Caesar, he saw his sister in a relaxed state in the chambers and ran off completely enraged. This could have been jealousy either over his sister's affections or her own brilliant strategizing. Either way, Ptolemy XIII stormed out of the palace in a fit of rage, yelling about being betrayed by his sister and attempting to stir up a mob to defeat Cleopatra and Julius Caesar.

Despite these attempts, Caesar was a great speaker and was able to calm the crowd down by presenting Ptolemy Auletes' will, which stated that the brother and sister should have the throne together. He also officially named their even younger siblings (Arsinoe and Ptolemy XIV) as the rulers of an area Rome had recaptured not long before that, Rhodes. The decision to give Rhodes back to Egypt was not taken well by the citizens of Rome, but it was a strategic move by Julius set forth with the intentions of buying more time, securing his new lover's gratitude and undermining Ptolemy XIII and Pothinus' possible attempts to rebel against him by stirring up mobs.

The Banquet of Julius Caesar and the Dangerous Turn it took

Julius Caesar decided to hold a banquet to celebrate the decision of appointing the siblings as joint rulers. He had the displeasure, however, of discovering that Pothinus and Achillas were planning to defeat him. In response to this discovery, Caesar commanded that the banquet hall be surrounded by his army men and had Pothinus executed right then and there. Achillas, Ptolemy's general who had been helping him plan to defeat Caesar, was able to escape and rally Ptolemy's troops (only freshly back from Pelusium) and the Greeks of Alexandria who made up the guard of the town. The army had the palace surrounded but Julius, aware of the fact that he was in a tough spot, stayed indoors with his lover Cleopatra holding a hostage; Ptolemy XIII.

Caesar was aware of the fact that he was seriously outnumbered but he knew that he had aid on its way to help him- reinforcements from the Levant and Anatolia. In addition to this he was aware that Achillas would attempt to prevent them from helping, so as he organized a last minute defense of his palace he gave an order that every ship in the harbor be set on fire.

The flames reached warehouses on the nearby shorelines and Arsinoe, Cleopatra's sister, was able to escape with Ganymedes her tutor. Arsinoe then joined up with Achillas who succeeded to name her Egypt's Queen. She quickly responded to this by having him murdered when he disagreed with a decision she made, and replacing him with Ganymedes.

As the chaos continued outside the palace, Ganymedes plotted to poison the supply of water to Caesar's palace and arranged a way to cut the palace off using road blocks. However Cleopatra was aware of all of the local water course locations and the newer wells were cut off quickly. Caesar chose a tactical move of allowing Ptolemy to go free, hoping that Arsinoe and Ptolemy would fight and both become weakened. Unfortunately for Julius the siblings were able to look past their rivalry with the goal of defeating Caesar and Cleopatra in mind, which only strengthened the army of Ptolmy and the guard of Alexandria.

At this point we can assume that Cleopatra was getting a bit concerned about her luck running out, but it appears that Julius never even considered giving her over to the enemies for his own benefit. The reasons for this are uncertain; it could have been due to his own bravery but many believe that it was mostly because he had recently found out that Cleopatra was pregnant and expecting a son.

The Dramatic Closing of the Battle at the Palace

Things were looking dire for the couple, but just when everything appeared to be looking too bad the reinforcements of Caesar showed up and engaged in an intense battle. After this they took over the causeway which lined the Great Lighthouse to Caesar's palace. Just then another wave of reinforcements appeared, the army of the Prince of Pergamon, and Caesar had further support. This meant that Ptolemy had no choice but to go south and face the army.

Julius led his army out to pursue, teaming up with his allies of Pergamon and engaging in a battle which led to Ptolemy being drowned and defeated in the Nile River. Upon his death, Julius retrieved Ptolemy's body from the Nile and began heading to the capital city of Alexandria to make Cleopatra aware of his success. She showed up to meet him, leading an impressive procession of gods and sacred symbols. Rumors say that she was dressed up to emulate Isis, her favorite goddess, and was no doubt stunning to behold.

Upon meeting his lover, Julius Caesar officially named her younger sibling Ptolemy XIV as the ruler alongside her. This would ensure that her right to the throne was secure. After this he married her in the typical Egyptian way, but their union was not considered official in Rome since he had already been married to someone else and it was considered illegal for citizens of Rome to marry someone from another country.

The Celebration Following the Marriage of Julius and Cleopatra

The newlyweds took a cruise down the Nile River to celebrate their honeymoon. This gave Cleopatra an opportunity to show the Egyptian people that she was completely in charge and also for her to show her new husband her homeland. This honeymoon cruise was probably also meant to be a journey toward the land of Edfu, where she could establish a connection between her young son Caesarion and the god Horus, which would ensure his fate as the leader of Egypt in the future.

As the couple began their return to the capital city of Alexandria, Julius started to plan his return to his homeland of Rome. The citizens of his homeland criticized him quite harshly for his failure to take over Egypt and add it to the empire. They also criticized Caesar for staying in Egypt for too long after Ptolemy XIII's death in the river. In Rome there were quite a few factions who had maintained their loyalty to the fallen Pompey, some of whom involved his own sons. This meant that the ruler had a lot of matters of importance he needed to handle, including the necessity of visiting his Jewish allies and showing them appreciation for the support they provided during the war of Alexandria.

The ruler abandoned not one but three different legions in the capital city so he could support his wife, Cleopatra, while she established the status of Egypt and also to take Arsinoe as a prisoner back to Rome with him for her treasonous ways. In addition to this he handed over Cyprus to Cleopatra, which gave her the revenue necessary to lower taxes in Egypt while improving the economy at the same time.

The Birth of Their Son, Caesarion

Cleopatra had her son, Ptolemy XV Caesarion, in the summer of 47 B.C. In honor of this there was a decree set up in a specific version of hieroglyphs in Saqqara. In addition to this, the baby's lineage was announced and written on buildings and monuments across the nation (the Temple of Dendera was among these, depicting a famous scene). Julius appears to have been overjoyed at the birth of his son. Some people who worked under Caesar started looking into the idea of adjusting Roman law to assign his new son as the rightful heir, searching for ways around the laws against marrying people from different countries and his previous marriage.

Julius had a coin made that depicted the goddesses Aphrodite and Venus, and his wife Cleopatra also had a coin made that showed herself as Aphrodite and Venus nursing her new baby, Caesarion. In the year 46 B.C. she went to Rome, accompanied by her husband and brother, Ptolemy XIV, and her son (who Julius was still having a hard time getting recognized as his rightful heir to the throne).

They were all welcomed officially as allies and friends of the people of Rome, and assigned a villa at the Hill of Janiculum to live in which belonged to Caesar. The villa was very large and had a nice view of the nearby city and a fabulous garden area. Caesar did not live here with them however, and stayed with his original Roman wife, Calpurnia.

Since the Egyptian marriage between Julius and Cleopatra was not officially recognized by the law of Rome, Cleopatra became known as his mistress instead of his wife. She held multiple "symposia", where many people were invited to come and enjoy feasts and live poetry which was said to have made her popular with the friends of her husband. Cleopatra also seems to have had something to do with Mark Antony returning to the good graces of Caesar. He had been the deputy of Julius, but Lepidus was assigned to replace him due to his questionable and immoral habits. This could have been aided by the fact that Mark Antony enjoyed Greek culture and style and was rumored to be close with the Ptolemys.

Caesar's Choices for Statues and their Significant Placement

Julius had made a promise that stated that if he were to prevail against his enemy Pompey, he would erect a brand new temple to honor his divine ancestor, Venus Genetrix. Caesar put a statue made of bronze which depicted Alexander the Great's horse, Bucephalus, out in front of this structure and also had a gold statue of his lover, Cleopatra, placed next to the Venus statue in the middle of this temple.

It was not unusual for pharaohs of the Ptolemaic era to have statues depicting themselves placed right next to deities, but the practices of Rome were quite different and did not approve of placing a human's form alongside gods. This seemed to claim that she possessed special authority of a divine nature, which they did not approve of.

Also the goddess Venus was typically used to represent marriage, and the Roman citizens saw his choice of the Venus statue as an indirect but obvious statement about his marriage to Cleopatra. Julius also made sure to put statues depicting himself throughout Rome, including at the Romulus (the man who discovered Rome and was thus deified) temple.

Another state was titled "unvanquished god", a term people typically reserved for the revered Alexander the Great. Caesar was in charge of a large amount of construction activity, which usually involved the classic Egyptian-Greek hybrid style and set his mind to erecting a giant Roman library to rival the biggest library that existed at the time (the Alexandrian Great Library).

Cleopatra's Irreplaceable Impacts on Roman Culture

The astronomers employed by Cleopatra aided Julius in creating the Julian calendar, which had never existed previously and was intended to take the place of the Roman calendar (which was rumored to be defective). The Julian calendar was to have a leap year and 365 days and is what we base our current, modern calendar on o(with only small changes made by Pope Gregory, many years later). It is unquestionable that Cleopatra had a huge and unrivaled effect on the culture and art of Rome.

Regardless of these positive contributions to the culture of Rome, the relationship of Caesar and Cleopatra was not very popular with the senate of Rome. Calpurnia came from a strong and popular family in Rome and was demure and subservient, as was typical of Roman women at the time. Cleopatra on the other hand was the opposite; outspoken, ambitious and powerful. Julius had countless enemies during this time period, Cicero the orator being the main one and possibly the most menacing threat to him.

Cicero the orator officially named Alexandria as the home to all deceit and tricks, and made no secret of the fact that he hated Cleopatra. Cicero believed that females were inherently weak on an intellectual level and should look to and be under the guidance of their superior male guardians. For this reason, he was very unsettled about Caesar being so heavily influenced by Cleopatra.

Around this time, rumors began circulating that Julius had plans to switch the capital over to Alexandria; in essence adding to the power of Egypt at the expense of Rome. In response to these rumors, senators started coming up with plans for reversing the reforms of Caesar.

Julius Caesar and his Contributions to the City

It was the year 45 B.C. when Julius came upon Pompey's sons and had an intense and bloody battle with them that ended in his favor. Regardless of this success, the youngest son of Pompey was able to escape and Julius experienced a number of seizures in quick succession. These seizures concerned him quite a bit and motivated him to retire to Lavicum to live in his villa and start rewriting his will. He made sure to leave a few golden coins to each citizen of Rome and established the luxurious villa gardens at the hill of Janiculum as public park property.

He also left some of his wealth to Mark Antony and his nephew, Octavian. Though he had tried many times, he had still been unable to change Roman law to include his son Caesarion or wife Cleopatra in the will, but made sure to start a clause which assigned guardians to children who would be born in the future. This is thought to have been included because Cleopatra was pregnant again at this time.

As he headed toward Rome, he decided to stop and spend a couple of days with the orator, Cicero, in order to acquire information about the senate's opinion of his new changes.

The senate had decided to name him as a lifelong dictator, but he wanted to go even further than this.

Caesar had plans to get rid of the Parthians (drawing inspiration from the famous Alexander the Great and his dreams), but an oracle of Sybelline clearly stated that this feat could only be undertaken by a king and Julius obviously wished for that title. Julius then went on to become the very first Roman citizen (who was still living) to have his face etched on a coin. On this coin he was given the prestigious title of the fatherland's father and started plotting on ways to become king at the upcoming celebration of Lupercalia Festival.

Caesar's Failed Attempts at Becoming King and the Dire Consequences

Caesar gave Mark Antony orders to go search for a crown and, once he found one, set it upon Julius' head. The plan was that Caesar would humbly refuse this honor but become convinced by the crowd's encouragement and enthusiasm. The plan seemed safe enough, but unfortunately it didn't go as planned. The crowd instead ended up cheering for his staged rejection of the title of king and the crown that was to come along with it. Slightly marred by this rejection, Caesar started preparing for his upcoming fight against the Parthians but his secret plans had been made obvious to the watching senate members, and even more plotting began to occur.

Julius Caesar did not survive this plotting and was murdered in 44 B.C. on what would then after be known as the Ides of March. His murderers had been hoping that the people of Rome would approve of the murder that had just taken place, but soon discovered that the opposite was true. Upon hearing

festivals, fancy dinners and other extravagant affairs, getting drunk off wine. These reports did not help his reputation in Rome one bit. One account of his unpopularity stated that he was a fine man with great abilities, but was driven away from his Roman roots by drunkenness and his infatuation with Cleopatra.

Regardless of the fun he was having in Egypt, Mark Antony needed to go back to Rome at some point and when he returned the nation was split in thirds. Lepidus, Octavian and Antony were the three generals ruling over the empire. Part of the agreement of a settlement in this arrangement was that Mark would be married off to Octavian's sister, Octavia. This was likely more about political gains than it was about love, but it probably still bothered Cleopatra. The next year she had a set of twins named Cleopatra Selene II and Alexander Helios.

Octavia Depicted as the Goddess

In the year 39 B.C. Antony and Octavia had a child named Antonia and coins were created to depict the symbolically significant relationship of Mark Antony and Octavia as the goddess of Athens. It's been said that Octavia had intentions of supplanting Cleopatra and saw her as useful in a political sense since she was keeping peace between her brother and father for the time being. Mark Antony's wife convinced him to gift 130 ships to Octavian in exchange for 20,000 army men to aid Mark in his battle with the Parthians.

In the year 37 B.C., Mark headed East with his wife. At this time Octavia was expecting their second baby and the long trip was difficult for her, so she headed back home to Rome where her brother would look out for her. Not long after this, it became obvious to Mark Antony that her brother had no intentions of living up to his promise to send out troops and that his best bet was to get Cleopatra's help. It had been four years since he had seen her, and in those years he had gotten married to someone else, had two children and still had never seen his own children with Cleopatra.

The Reunion of Mark Antony and Cleopatra

Later on that same year, Antony asked Cleopatra to come with him to Antioch where the two were wedded. Although there were probably emotional reasons for this marriage, there were undeniable political advantages to this union. The marriage prompted them both to look past the fact that they had been apart for a few years and also the fact that Antony was married already. It's impossible to know for sure how much love had to do with their decision to get married, but we can know for sure that Antony gifted land to Cleopatra which was equal to nearly the entire territory the dynasty of Egypt had held at its highest point.

Cleopatra made her way back to her home nation, joyfully triumphant, and decided to stay in Jerusalem for a while. Here she had a harsh rivalry and her assassination was planned by Herod. When he was convinced, however, that he could never successfully murder her and get away with it he decided to try to ruin her reputation by spreading rumors that Cleopatra had attempted to seduce him, but the rumors held no water.

By the year 36 B.C. Cleopatra had made it back to the capital city of Egypt, and was powerful and rich. She made Caesarion her co-ruler and had her third baby, who she named Ptolemy Philadephus. Though this was probably a joyful time for the new mother, her husband Antony was not doing very well in Parthia. He had been abandoned by his allies and forced to back off, with a quarter of his men getting lost to hunger and sickness. Octavian sent his sister, Octavia, to bring Antony supplies, but only delivered a small portion of the reinforcements he had originally promised Antony.

An Important Decision for Mark Antony

Octavian was well aware that if Antony met up with Octavia, it would cause problems between Cleopatra and him. He also knew that if Antony did not go he would become even more distant from his homeland of Rome, where his relationship with Cleopatra was unpopular and illegal. Mark Antony had a difficult choice to make and ended up opting for his wife, Cleopatra, and sent Octavia back home to Octavian, her brother, in Rome.

Mark Antony enjoyed triumph in the country of Armenia not long after this and decided to celebrate this victory in Egypt's capital city, Alexandria, instead of his home nation of Rome. This decision was viewed as Mark Antony's intention to relocate to Alexandria. During this time Octavian also held a celebration, most likely attempting to celebrate his absence. At this time, Octavia got an exciting promotion. She rose to Vestal Virgin status and had a statue of herself erected, right next to a statue in the Forum erected for Antony.

Changes Made by the Couple in Egypt

While celebrating his victories in Alexandria, Antony officially established Cleopatra as the ultimate queen of queens. He also named himself as the son of Caesar, and not Octavian. He announced too that Caesarion and Cleopatra would jointly rule over both Cyprus and Egypt. In addition to this, he announced that Media's ruler would henceforth be Alexander Helios. In return for this grand favor, his wife Cleopatra aided him in his battle against the Parthians by paying for a huge fleet to assist him.

At this point, the bitter relationship between Octavian and Mark Antony was coming to a head, and Octavian started a campaign with intentions of ruining Antony's reputation even further. This involved spreading rumors all over Rome about the ill intentions Cleopatra and Antony had and trying to frame their marriage in a negative way. This began an increasingly negative feud in which Antony was accused of abandoning his homeland and wife for a foreign nation and woman. Rumors of Octavian were spread which claimed that he was a coward and a homosexual.

Regardless of the smear campaign, Mark Antony had decent and loyal connections in Rome and appeared to have won the feud when a couple of his friends were given government authority. How much he had really given Cleopatra was made known to senate members and Antony suggested that he would give over his ruling privileges on one condition; Octavian must also give over his. Octavian's response was not positive and he threw out threats, insults and even brought armed forced inside the meeting area of the senate.

Luxurious Fleets and Smear Campaigns

Mark Antony's government friends and many of the senate members decided to leave Rome and head to Ephesus to start a new senate. Here Cleopatra joined them accompanied by riches and an extensive fleet, along with a huge number of Greek troops. Cleopatra and Antony made their way to the capital of Greece to face the music and also so that Antony could attempt to divorce his previous wife, Octavia. It was clear that Octavian needed to take action soon, but he had no desire to begin yet another battle so he instead focused his energies on smearing the name of Cleopatra, claiming that she was a huge threat to the Roman people and wanted to ruin their home.

He also set about smearing Antony's name, depicting him as a wimpy traitor to his homeland who had been taken advantage of by an evil and corrupt woman. This campaign for smearing the couple's names was quite successful and led to Cleopatra being officially named Rome's enemy, with a war declaration being initiated against her. Although this made how the Romans felt about her clear, Mark Antony's name was nowhere to be found in this declaration.

Agrippa commanded a fleet of Rome and met Cleopatra and Antony's fleets near Actium. The victory this time went to Octavian. Cleopatra took this chance to escape back to Egypt, worried that officials might get confident about defeating her after hearing that they had lost. Instead she pretended as though she had won and even garnered her ship to make it appear that she had and scare away any potential attackers.

Mark Antony soon after made his way to Africa looking for reinforcements or allies, but he didn't find help there and had to return to the capital city of Egypt. Cleopatra offered Octavian a crown which was meant to signify that she was handing the kingdom over to him. In response to this he threatened to take her throne from her, but in secret told her that he would allow her to keep her position if she would only murder Mark Antony. Antony tried his best to defend Alexandria, but ended up killing himself instead of succumbing to becoming a prisoner of Rome.

Reports state that Antony stabbed himself with his own sword and that Cleopatra held him as he died. She was captured soon after and returned to Octavian, who had plans to bring her to Rome to be a slave. He also had intentions of executing her in a ritualistic style to celebrate his triumph, but his hopes of doing this would not come true.

Chapter 6:
The Results of her Alliances and Legacy

The alliances Cleopatra formed with both Mark Antony and Caesar temporarily brought restoration from the authority of Egypt, the empire her ancestors built, as well as relief from the constant concern of the Romans and the threat they brought. Cleopatra was also able to fix the troubled state of the kingdom and its inner-workings. She was willing to take any measures necessary to prevail, even over her siblings, and consequently struggled ruthlessly for her right to the throne as well as proclaiming Caesarion as a pharaoh at the time. The latter created a real possibly for a succession that was peaceful rather than difficult, which had long since been believed impossible.

Tumultuous Times in Egypt and how Cleopatra Responded

Cleopatra had many ambitious goals for her country, but they came with a considerable amount of risk. Her ambitions were possible, but not without extra help outside of Egypt itself. Her deceased dad's hard earned experiences had shown her that in order to gain success protectors and patrons of Rome must be in your good graces, but unfortunately for her this was not the case.

Cleopatra became widely known for her impressive claim of her right to the throne and was able to gain many benefits from her alliance with Caesar, but soon discovered that both were under threat. In the year 43 B.C., a civil war was renewed which created an urgency for her choosing a brand new patron from the Second Triumvirate.

Intelligent strategizing along with the unrelenting hostility Octavian felt toward Caesarion resulted in Mark Antony being chosen. The campaigns that he tried to run (such as the Parthian campaign) would point to the fate of her future as well as the fate of Egypt as a whole. For the remainder of this great historical period, the Roman Empire would take over Egypt as a province. The ruler Octavian along with a few that followed him were given the title of pharaoh, but emperors of Rome did not bother to rule there much or even travel to the country.

The Symbol of Cleopatra in History

Historical accounts of Cleopatra may be quite biased, but she became an unquestioned symbol. Statues of her were maintained, and the cult of Egypt that existed in her honor lived on for many years after her passing. However the power of how she would be known and seen for the rest of time was in the hands not of the Egyptians, but of the Romans.

The image the Romans put forth of Cleopatra began with a harsh campaign of propaganda started by Octavian with tactical motives. This played a huge role in how negatively she would come to be received or spoken of. History has shown us time and time again that simple propaganda is the most effective, so Octavian took advantage of this and focused on Cleopatra's supposed seduction of Antony and her evil plot to lure him from his homeland. He also spread the rumor that she did not have the best intentions at heart for Egypt, but instead wanted to seize power for selfish reasons using her manipulated husband, Mark Antony.

Octavian decided what this conflict would mean, and decided to prioritize the values and culture of Italy. If the "evil" plans of Cleopatra were to be successful, he had concerns that Romans could start to degenerate and act more like people from Egypt. Luckily, he told the Roman people, Cleopatra's plans were not successful and Octavian defeated her, rescuing the destiny of Rome and Italy as a whole.

Not only did this propaganda continue after Cleopatra passed, but it got even more intense. However it took on a new character and focus. Rather than hailing Cleopatra as a threat that needed to be conquered, she became known as a symbolic representation of anyone who would dare question the new order Octavian had worked hard to set forth.

Once she was gone, an immediate transformation started taking place. Octavian was now in charge of Egypt, and with this came a great responsibility to influence the attitudes of those he was ruling over. These changes took place following the passing of Cleopatra. He made sure to put his new image of the queen on display after his return to his home country in 29 B.C. Similar to what Caesar did in the year 46 B.C., Octavian triumphed over Egypt and decided to throw a huge celebration to commemorate his victory. At this Cleopatra's spirit permeated and was present as a symbol. He then had a monument built to celebrate his defeat of the ambitious queen.

More Propaganda from Octavian

This monument showed scenes of his victory and coins were created to celebrate his huge win, showing the head of Octavian and traditional symbols of Egypt. Other great things came of the propaganda Octavian spread, such as genius works of literature that would go on to become very famous and embody the spirit of the times. The written works commemorated the closing of a strong era and the return to peace for Rome.

Many of these works of literature spread the same type of propaganda that Octavian was set on spreading, portraying the fallen queen as a manipulator who took advantage of poor Antony. They wrote about his fate being sealed as soon as he laid eyes on her beauty. Some of the literature also claimed that every mistake Mark Antony made during those times was directly the fault of Cleopatra and his love for her.

The symbol of the fallen queen became a grand representation of a challenging rival to Octavian and all he represented. Everything written or spoken about her at that time claimed that she was a huge enemy, equally damaging and dangerous as other evil enemies. They claimed that she was overtaken by lust constantly and motivated by greed to become a powerful ruler. Nothing of her pure intentions in helping people was spoken of, and when it was it was downplayed severely.

Taking Octavian's example, many famous writers of that era took it upon themselves to craft a certain picture of Cleopatra the famous ruler. Certain stories of demonizing the queen became so repeated that they eventually became a lot more simplified than the reality of what happened. Her heroic aspects were often ignored and she was blamed constantly for things that were not necessarily her fault. She was even called Egypt's shame; harsh words to describe the ruler.

This ruthless picture of Cleopatra remained and became even more widely spread because it supported already existing fears and prejudices that people had. Many men lived in fear of the threat that a powerful woman could pose to the status quo they had grown accustomed to. Admitting to the power that Cleopatra possessed meant owning up to the dangers that the traditional social and gender roles were facing. The fears of Roman citizens at the time around cultural and ethnic differences did nothing to help this extreme fear.

The image of the famous queen has been portrayed countless times throughout history since the era of her ruling, in books and in countless films. Not all of these were hostile representations, but it's fair to say that most were. For example, Shakespeare was fair in his portrayal of her as a well-rounded woman with noble desires and dreams. There is something to be said for the differing motivations that drive the portrayals of impactful historical figures, and Cleopatra is no exception to this phenomenon. Once someone has passed on, the power lies in the hands of those who remain to draw whatever picture of the person they desire, and motivations are not always pure.

Cleopatra struggled long and hard to free her home nation of Egypt and even stood up for under-represented and less fortunate groups of differing ethnic and social classes. She volunteered herself as a symbol for these people and often had goals that were beneficial not just to her but to everyone in the nation. Unsurprisingly Cleopatra became somewhat of a feminist icon in some circles, since she acted on her own in a time when this was not common for women. She displayed goals that were far ahead of her time and set the stage for future events and equality movements for women. Multiple people have tried to claim descent from Cleopatra, including an Arab queen by the name of Palmyra who took over Egypt.

As mentioned briefly at the beginning of the book, disputes have occurred over Cleopatra's race and some African American groups have grasped the possibility that she was actually black, though other sources claim that that was impossible. Regardless of what race she actually was, the woman is an inspiring symbol for people of all colors and backgrounds. Her impact was the same regardless of the color of her skin, and we can all draw inspiration from her example, even in today's modern world.

A New City's Birth

It's no secret that the destiny of cities often had much to do with the destiny of the rulers that led them. Just as the emperor of Rome, Augustus, was linked with Rome and Athens, Cleopatra is forever entwined with Alexandria, Egypt's great capital. She spent most of her existence here and it was where the events that would shape her all occurred. This woman's memory is timeless and will never fade from this place, even as centuries pass.

Sitting at the opening of the Canopic branch of the most famous river in Egypt, the Nile, near the delta's western edge, Alexandria was not only the very first but the most popular and timeless of the many foundations created by Alexander the Great. He began this city soon before departing Egypt in the year 331 B.C. Some debate has occurred over why he decided on this specific place, but most agree that he probably had multiple reasons. Countless benefits were offered by choosing this specific location.

The location offered very simple access to the close by Nile River and also the inner parts of the entire country of Egypt. During this time period, ease of travel was extremely important and was one of the first things people looked for when they sought places to settle. For this reason, Alexandria appealed to people from far and wide. The city rested close to the famous Naukratis, a Greek city, which acted as the important link to be used by Greek and Egyptian citizens to travel back and forth between the countries.

The interest of Alexander the Great was also sparked, however, by Pharos which was just offshore from the city. This was where one of his all-time favorite and most inspiring stories took place, the *Odyssey*. This could have been a coincidence, but anyone who knows about Alexander the Great knows that he was heavily influenced by this work and likely considered that in his choice for where to place the capital city of Egypt. The city had its own irreplaceable spot in the world of Hellenistic times. It's true that it was created around a settlement in Egypt that already existed and called itself Egypt's capital.

Regardless of these facts, Alexandria was not technically part of the nation of Egypt. Instead it was a city-state belonging to Greece with its very own land. The same as other similar city-states, citizenship of the area of Alexandria was only allowed to people from Macedonia or Greece, who Alexander the Great tried to encourage to come there and stay to settle. The groups that were encouraged to settle there only made up a small percentage of the total population of this place. There was also a quite free policy toward immigration which allowed for a richly varied population of differing ethnicities. These included Nubians, Syrians, Egyptians of course and even Jews, who ended up making up an entire fifth of the entire area.

The culturally rich community of Jews had a wonderful and majestic synagogue that was considered a great marvel, coming in second only behind Jerusalem's temple. This city was far ahead of its time as far as including different belief systems, people and religions went. The degree of openness displayed in this place would not be matched until many, many years later as humanity progressed.

The Ptolemies contributed largely to Alexandra by their patronage and the link between Africa, the Mediterranean, Arabia and other nations that lay on the border of the nearby Indian Ocean. This link also provided many commercial benefits to the inhabitants of the city which was greatly appreciated. When Cleopatra finally made her appearance on the throne in the year 50 B.C., this great city had exploded to half a million citizens and was considered the Mediterranean Basin's main, major city.

Chapter 7:
The Death of the Queen

Instead of giving Octavian the pleasure of taking her as prisoner and having her executed to parade his victory in front of onlookers, Cleopatra was determined to make her own fate. She made sure that she wouldn't be dragged through the Roman streets right before being executed in a humiliating fashion, and responded to this threat by plotting her own suicide.

Cleopatra started to test out poisons on people to figure out which one she would prefer to use. It wasn't average citizens she did this on, however, but prisoners who already had life sentences. After doing these experiments, she ended up realizing that these quick poisons would be too painful for her and that the ones that weren't too painful acted far too slowly for what she needed. This gave her the idea of using animal venom instead.

The Famed Snakebite Death of Cleopatra

Once Cleopatra had made the choice to use animal venom for her own death, the specific option was obvious; an asp bite. During this time she worked on the place she would spend the rest of eternity; her mausoleum. She made sure to leave explicit mummification instructions to those around her to ensure that she would have a dignified burial and afterlife.

When Cleopatra's fleet of ships was overtaken by those of Octavian, she had immediately jumped to the worst conclusion and headed, with her servants, for her waiting tomb. She was accompanied by her servants and gave them explicit instructions that they should tell anyone who asked about Cleopatra that she had died already. At this point Mark Antony was still alive and had come back to find her at the palace. He was given the fake news that she had died already and, at that moment, impaled himself on his own sword calling out his despair at losing his loved one and reason to live.

At this point, he was seriously injured but had not died. Finally he was given the news that Cleopatra was not, in fact, dead, and her servants helped him over to her tomb where she was waiting. The door to the tomb was sealed shut so he had to be taken up to the window using a rope to haul his wounded body. As soon as she set eyes upon him, the queen started mourning him in a very dramatic fashion that was customary, by cutting her own body and smearing his blood over her hands and face and also beating herself on the chest. Antony, though wounded, tried his best to console her and they both had a last drink together before he passed away while she held him.

Octavian was worried that Cleopatra was going to commit suicide and possibly set her valuable treasures aflame, so he gave his men orders to keep her responsive and talking. They also gave her false promises about her son being able to rule over the nation of Egypt after she passed on. This created the necessary diversion for Octavian's men to sneak in and grab her, and she was then sentenced to a period of house arrest. Octavian made it his next goal to calm down the people of Alexandria and also to closely look over Alexander the Great's tomb, hoping that the treasure of Ptolemy was still inside.

The son of Mark Antony was found murdered by beheading in the Caesareum and all three of Cleopatra's kids were taken and held as captives. As all of this was happening Octavian took the opportunity to take the leftover treasures inside the

Caeasareum, as well as the riches hidden inside of the tomb of Cleopatra. He also took this opportunity to closely inspect Mark Antony's dead body.

Distraught at everything crashing down around her Cleopatra was in an extreme state of mourning, hurting herself so severely that she developed a fever from the deepness of her wounds. Cleopatra wouldn't eat anything at all in her grief but in response to this, Octavian threatened to hurt her kids if she didn't start taking care of herself and recovering. This was due to the fact that he wished to feature her in his victory and make it all the more dramatic and impressive.

It has been suggested that Cleopatra might have been killed by him instead of killing herself, but no evidence exists for this supposition. Also, although she was a symbol of rebellion against all Octavian stood for and represented he had the perfect opportunity to let her die of natural causes which he didn't take, so we can safely rule out that theory altogether.

Some stories state that Cleopatra tried to seduce Octavian when he went to see her after she had gotten better but again, there is no evidence for this assumption. Others assume that the meeting didn't actually happen in the first place. In the late summer of 30 B.C. Cleopatra was able to officially say goodbye to Antony. For this event she took a bath, wore her absolute finest clothes and adornments and made sure she looked impeccable. After this, she dismissed everyone around her except for two of her friends and servants who were allowed to stay, wrote a farewell note with the request that she be buried alongside the deceased Mark Antony and then killed herself.

Although other aspects of her life are matters of dispute, historians agree that Cleopatra committed suicide via an asp bite. The snake was smuggled into the area where she was by a clever and willing accomplice. An asp bite is said to be a very painful and slow means of dying, but it was recorded that Cleopatra's death was fast and quite peaceful. It's been rumored that the two close friends of hers that were there while she died also committed suicide shortly after her, using the same poison as Cleopatra.

The Aftermath of the Death of the Queen

When the men of Octavian burst into the chambers to discover the dead body of Cleopatra, one of her loyal servants was in the middle of arranging upon her head a crown so that she could die adorned and the servant died shortly after. Some might assume that the death of Cleopatra would end her legacy, but this is far from true. She may have even become more famous after her passing since countless legends have been written and spoken about her life. Her influence is not something that could have faded with something as simple as death. The legacy this fearless leader and tactical ruler left behind will live on forever.

Her death also did not signify that her family would end, since she had multiple children. She had the pair of twins, Alexander Helios and Cleopatra Selene, and Ptolemy Philadelphos, all with Mark Antony. She also had, of course, the baby of Julius Caesar, Caesarion. It is true that Octavian executed poor Caesarion, but he did not murder Ptolemy or the twins- luckily for her. Although she lost her kingdom in the end, at least her legacy lived on through her bloodline.

Conclusion

Thank you again for downloading this book!

I hope this book was able to help you to get a better understanding of the important and famous historical figure, Cleopatra. With so many sources of historical information out there, it's hard to know what to trust. This book was created with the intention of delivering the truest depiction of historical events concerning the queen, Cleopatra.

It is important to look to history for insight into our personal lives and humanity as a whole. There are countless valuable lessons to be learned from fearless leaders who shaped history. The next step is to observe your own life and find out how the story of Cleopatra can inspire you to be stronger and improve yourself.

Finally, if you enjoyed this book, then I'd like to ask you for a favour- would you be kind enough to leave a review for this book on Amazon? It'd be greatly appreciated!

Click here to leave a review for this book on Amazon!

Thank you and good luck!

Preview Of Ancient Egypt

A Guide to the Gods, Pharaohs, Dynasties and Traditions of Ancient Egypt

Introduction

What makes Egypt so fascinating to us that there is a branch of archaeology called Egyptology? What did the ancient Egyptian culture have that makes it worth studying? Sun, sand, and pyramids await visitors in Egypt today, but what about the civilizations Egypt was built on? What did they find 5000 years ago to make them want to build a life in Egypt? To understand Ancient Egypt, one must also have a basis in time. When did the first settlers arrive in Egypt? When were the first pyramids erected? When did the first Pharaoh start ruling Egypt as a country in its own right? All of these questions and more will be answered for you, to help you understand that sometimes history has lessons for us- perhaps forgotten lessons that need to be brought back.

A Timeline of Ancient Egypt

Ancient Egypt is considered to be the period in time from 5000 BC to 332 BC. Little is known about the pre-dynastic period because few records exist. However, the period lasted for nearly 2000 years. Civilizations cropped up around the Nile and in Northern Africa along other water sources. These communities were based on agriculture and hunting. Trade between the groups occurred in order to share resources, and it opened the way for arts and crafts, politics, religion, and technology to develop.

Approximately 300 years before the pre-dynastic period ended in 3100, two kingdoms rose to power. One was called the Red Land, which was in the north of Egypt along the Nile River Delta, perhaps extending as far as what is now Atfih. The other kingdom was the White Land in the south, which was probably the area between Atfih and Gebel es-Silsila.

Did you know: Hollywood movies like The Mummy and The Mummy Returns are based on facts pulled from Ancient Egyptian history. The King of the southern kingdom was known as Scorpion. Scorpion tried to conquer the Red Land in 3200BC. However, he was not successful.

It was a century later before the two kingdoms would become one under King Menes. King Menes assumed the title of Pharaoh, which meant King in Egyptian, and he ruled over the first dynasty of Egypt.

King Menes began the Archaic Period, which lasted from 3100 to 2686 BC. King Menes lived and ruled Egypt in White Walls. White Walls, now called Memphis, was the capital of Ancient Egypt. It rests on the apex of the Nile River's delta. It was this capital that arose as a metropolis, dominating Egyptian society during the Old Kingdom Period. It was this period that was responsible for founding the Egyptian Society, the ideology of kingship and the religious beliefs in the gods like Horus. Irrigation, fertilization and better farming were discovered during this period.

Egypt is broken into periods by archaeologists. The next periods were as follows:

- Old Kingdom - 2686 to 2181 BC

- First Intermediate Period - 2181 to 2055 BC

- Middle Kingdom – The 12th Dynasty - 2055 to 1786 BC

- Second Intermediate Period - 1786 to 1567 BC

- New Kingdom - 1567 to 1085 BC

- Third Intermediate Period - 1085 to 664 BC

- Late Period - 664 to 332 BC

Most of the following chapters will concentrate on the Old Kingdom period. It is the age of the pyramid builders, and it is also considered the third dynasty of Pharaohs. You might recognize a few names from this period such as Imhotep, who was highlighted in the Hollywood films. King Djoser was ruling at the time and asked Imhotep to create a funerary monument for him. The result was the Step-Pyramid at Saqqara.

For the third and fourth dynasties, Egypt was considered a place of prosperity and peace. It was also the time when most of the pyramids were built. This age started to end towards the 5th and 6th dynasties, and the wealth of the King was starting to disappear due to the expensive pyramid building. Power was also starting to falter for the Pharaohs with more nobility and priests taking over the power stating that the Sun God Ra was the true power. At the end of the 6th dynasty King Pepy II died. He was in rule for nearly 94 years.

The period Egyptologists call Ancient Egypt ended when Alexander the Great defeated the Persian Empire. Alexander ruled Egypt until his death then Ptolemy took over control, leaving his descendants in charge. The last Ptolemaic Egyptian ruler was Cleopatra VII - she surrendered to Octavian, known later as Augustus in 31 BC, leaving Egypt under Roman rule for six centuries. When Arabs defeated Roman rulers in the 7th century AD, Islam was introduced to the country and most of the Egyptian way of life disappeared.

Egypt was not the only civilization to be advancing in 5000 BC. Numerous cultures around the world started to settle, to use their own concepts of agriculture and to trade between various cities as trade routes started to open up. China, Egypt,

Europe, and even early civilizations in the Americas existed. But what fascinates us the most about the Ancient Egyptian culture is their advancement in various areas including agriculture, architecture, women's roles and politics. Think about how women are treated in certain cultures even today. Remember how recently American women won the right to vote, and then consider the daily life of Egyptians over 5000 centuries ago that you will learn about in this book.

Keep in mind these other cultures as you explore the daily life, pyramids, architecture, dynasties and Pharaohs of ancient Egypt. Consider what life might be like today if Egyptian ways of life had survived instead of being stamped out by Alexander the Great and the Islamic rule. It is the advancements of ancient Egypt that truly grab Egyptologists attention.

Chapter 1:
Daily Life in Ancient Egypt

Archaeology gives us a mere glimpse into the past of Ancient Egypt and the Egyptian lifestyle. Many tomb paintings and hieroglyphic texts offer a look into the elitist world, but barely provide any details of regular daily life. Many countries may have been run by Kings and Queens, but it was the peasantry that made up the trade, crafts and food supply any civilization ran on. It was the same for the Egyptians. Pharaohs provided rules and laws, but it was the peasants' daily activities that ensured the wealthy could truly live in comfort. If not for peasants running farms, creating crafts and becoming trades people, the wealthy would have had to spend time doing these 'mundane' chores.

It is difficult to determine the true daily life of regular Egyptians because many scribes wrote about the 'important' people of Egypt rather than the day to day people. However, there are certain things archaeologists have been able to surmise about life as a regular Egyptian.

Marriage

The Egyptians had to marry early in their lives. Living to an age of 40 for most was not possible, particularly in the peasant class. The lack of food, the excess of hard work, and the toll of the desert made it difficult for most to survive. There were a few Pharaohs who lived to be quite old- one in particular ruled for nearly 94 years, according to archaeological evidence. Most women would be married off when they came into maturity or childbearing age.

The Nuclear Family

A nuclear family or elementary family is one that consists of a pair of adults and their children. Many Egyptians had a nuclear family dynamic, where one man and one woman supported the family. This is not to say that the Egyptians were monogamous. Many marriages were polygamous; however there was always a chief wife who was higher in the hierarchy than any of the others and was responsible for the day to day running of the household.

The Husband's Role

The husband was the man responsible for the economic well-being of the family. He was the person who would go out and run the farm, hold a job or work for the wealthy.

The husband was raised to respect his father and to become a husband who would be obeyed by the wives he took. Men could be slaves, servants or craftsmen. Most craftsmen learned their trade from their fathers or from artisans willing to take on an apprentice.

The Wife's Role

Depending on whether the family had more than one wife, the role for the chief wife was always to run the household. Contrary to what one might think, women were treated with respect. They could have opinions, make statements and be treated as equals. More than a few daughters of powerful men held positions, such as Nefertiti and Cleopatra. In fact women could own property, conduct business like men and testify in court. Women would raise the children and prepare the meals, yet still be seen as equals.

It was a necessity in households to have more than one wife, not just a desire by the husband. Wives bore children, and children worked in the house and fields. The role of all the wives and not just the chief wife was to rear the children, and to help ensure they could live long and help their fathers. There would be times when more than one wife gave birth within a few days or months of another.

Children

A husband could have many children. They were a "blessing from the gods," especially in royal and noble families. Pictures left behind show King Akhenaten and Queen Nefertiti loving their six daughters.

Children played very little in Egypt. There are some remnants and pictures that show children playing sports and with handmade toys, but these children were more likely from wealthier families.

The children of peasants would have had to work when they were old enough to understand the job they needed to do. For male children, this was normally farming or apprenticing as a tradesman in their father's business. For female children, it was about learning the household - how to run it, how to make food and how to be a good wife. The cycle would continue, with the daughters finding husbands when they were of marriageable age, and the men working the fields until it was time to find wives and build their own family.

Children in wealthy families would be given an education. This formal education allowed privileged children to become army officers or scribes.

The Working Life

As with many cultures of this time period, there were definite class distinctions. Those who were born to privilege were able to live comfortable lives with slaves or servants to do their work. The peasants had to live using agricultural techniques to grow food such as wheat to survive. A few of the peasants were lucky enough to have grazing lands where they were able to raise meat; however, these peasants often needed to sell the meat they raised to subsist. This meant they ate the wheat and some of the meagre vegetables they could grow in the desert.

Some families were lucky enough to have ox-drawn plows for their plowing, planting and harvesting, but even then the life was a tough one.

Peasants could not hope to raise their class status. Marriage between different social classes was not acceptable in most instances. Additionally, the expense of living life was too great for peasants to be able to save money and raise their social class. Taxes were imposed on all crops because the land was owned by the King, and the peasants were granted the right to use it to make a life.

Scholars find it difficult to determine the true way of life for most peasants, slaves and servants because of contradictory texts and little available information. It has been theorized that slaves were more like servants in most households. Yet it is known that slave labor was used to build the pyramids, so there were people who worked in degrading and humiliating positions.

Food and Beverages

Besides wheat for food, most peasants relied on beer. It was brewed from barley, using processes very similar to the ones we have today. For higher classes, meat and wine were on the table. The other common food amongst all classes was bread. The bread was seasoned with honey, sesame seeds, fruit and herbs.

Dwellings

Clearly the Pharaohs and upper classes had palatial homes. The remnants of these homes in pictures and in ruins are easily seen today. Peasants were not as lucky with their homes. Most homes were adobe (building materials made from the earth and organic materials) to keep the interior of the homes cool in the hot sun. Sun dried mud was used to create the adobe exteriors, which had doors and windows covered with mats as a way to keep out insects and flies. For nobles, the home was divided into three parts: a reception area, private quarters and a hall.

Peasants had what would be considered town homes today, with two or three stories. The first floor of the town home was for business or receiving people. The top floor or two would be private housing based on the amount of family members the peasant had. The roofs of these buildings were flat, enabling Egyptians to sleep outdoors in the hotter months.

At first mud and papyrus were used to construct homes, but soon child labor using children from about 4 years old and up was used to create actual bricks for the adobe dwellings. In most cases, peasants had one room to live and sleep in, with a ramp or ladder to go from the bottom service area to the top floor or the roof.

The lack of plumbing meant sewage was dumped either in the rivers, or in the streets or pits. The downside was that the water Egyptians had to use to live with came from these rivers. The buckets would be used to bring water in for drinking, bathing and cooking, then either be tossed out into the streets, back into the rivers, or into pits constructed for sewage purposes.

There was one thing that made families lucky- if they were pyramid workers. Homes were provided for pyramid workers because these individuals were too busy working on giant structures for the Kings to be able to take care of the building of their own places.

Homes for Richer Families

It is known that richer families actually had stone houses, using materials such as granite, which could be locked from the inside. There have been keys that date to 1550 BC. These wealthier families painted their homes white to help keep the homes cooler during the day. Artists were often hired to paint the inside walls to bring a fresh look to the home. Some of the richest families had 30 rooms with even bathrooms inside, although these rooms lacked running water. Bars were used in richer homes to ensure wild animals and intruders remained outside. Master suites for the husband, along with a toilet area, were made in some of the richest homes. Pipes from gardens led into the bathroom to bring in fresh water, although it was not like the running water of today.

These rich homes held mirrors, pots, pans, shelves, beds, heat, fountains, lighting, cosmetics, perfume pots and various sets of clean clothing. A lot of the homes had gardens and pools containing fish, and flowers that could bloom in Egypt.

Wealthy households held parties, with plenty of food and beverages. Music was also incorporated into these parties. The children of these families had toys carved into shapes like horses, balls and animals. There were also a few board games called Hounds and Jackals, and Senet.

Daily Life and the Nile

Life revolved around the Nile for everyone. It didn't matter if a person was wealthy or not, the Nile was the best source of fish and water and was the easiest way to travel. Along the banks of the Nile were rich areas of fertile soil that were necessary to help people survive.

Each year for three months, the Nile would flood. The waters would fill the crop land with much needed water, allowing the wheat and other crops to grow. It also ensured villages and cities could be built around the Nile.

The Nile provided papyrus reeds. Some families took these reeds to make paper or building materials. When the water receded, they still had the ability to get water into buckets and back to the cities and villages.

Fashion in Daily Life

For men, children and women, clothing was a necessity because of the hot sun. Some children just had enough cloth to cover their important areas, while wealthier families would wear robes made of linen, which also included headdresses. Makeup was also a part of everyday life, no matter the class because it helped protect peoples' skin from the damage sun could do.

Bathing was important as a daily ritual, either in the river or in bath basins at home. Cleansing cream made with lime, oil and perfume was used rather than soap, but they were able to keep clean and hygienic.

Jewelry was just as important to people as the clothing worn. Amulets and rings for religious purposes were worn by most Egyptians; even peasants had simple earrings, amulets and bracelets. Wealthier families had beaded collars, pendants and jewelry of Electrum, silver and gold.

When you consider the daily life of peasants and wealthier Egyptians there are certain cultural lessons to be learned.

- Women were respected, unlike certain cultures of today – a far contrast between the fights for the rights to vote that happened in European and American cultures in more modern day.

- Women may have borne children and run the households, but they also conducted business, were allowed in the courts and were important to the family dynamic.

- Bathing was a must, not something to be feared. Egyptians may not have understood hygiene the way we do now, but they knew using perfume was hardly enough to keep them clean. They bathed every day, unlike later European cultures.

Obviously, there were some deficiencies when it came to sewage and keeping their main water source clean of defecation, and using slave labor for building pyramids. However, it is difficult to argue with some methods Egyptians had in their daily life. They knew what could be grown in their area, how to keep their homes cooler and how to fish for protein. It did not take very long for better homes to be built, or for geometric shapes to be constructed that have lasted millennia for us to see.

Chapter 2:
Pyramids and Monuments of Egypt

The pyramids and monuments of Egypt that exist for tourists to see today were built over three millennia, by several dynastic rulers. Many of these structures have withstood the test of time- the sand, the sun and the sandstorms that may have obliterated entire groups of people did not destroy the structures. Unfortunately, not all structures remain in perfect condition. Pollution from tour buses and decades of exploration have all weakened the pyramids and monuments that exist in Egypt. There are even a few architectural wonders that have been covered and uncovered a few times due to sandstorms.

Step-Pyramid at Saqqara

Archaeologists also refer to this as the Step-Pyramid of Djoser, since he was the Pharaoh in charge of the first pyramid to be built. Its construction was designed specifically to inter Djoser upon his death. Originally the building was a flat roofed mastaba; however, when Imhotep finished the structure, it had increased to six layers and was what we now call a pyramid. It stood 204 feet high. Like the original mastaba tombs of earlier Egyptians, the burial chamber for Djoser is underground. There is a maze of tunnels that were hidden by the structure, but that have now been uncovered by archaeologists.

The Bent Pyramid

The Bent Pyramid or Southern Shining Pyramid was constructed during the 4th dynasty, circa 2600 BC. It stands 344 feet tall, with 617 feet at its base width. Pharaoh Snefru had this pyramid built 40 kilometers south of Cairo in Dahshur, which is known as the royal necropolis of Dashur. It was the second pyramid Snefru requested during his reign.

At first the pyramid begins a 54 degree angle, but this marvel became 43 degrees at the top giving it a bent appearance and thus its modern name. It is long believed by archaeologists that the pyramid was created by a transition from step pyramids to smooth sided pyramids, which lends to the change in angles. The Red Pyramid, which was the third to be constructed by Snefru's rule, is a complete 43-degree angle structure of smooth walls and is why most believe the Bent Pyramid was a transition between the two types of pyramids.

The Bent Pyramid is also considered unique because the outer limestone shell is mostly intact, which is very different from most of the other 90 pyramids and monuments. Scholars believe the limestone was undamaged over time because of the clearances between the outer casing and the expansion joints. The construction allowed for thermal expansion of the outer casing that other pyramids were unable to undergo.

Great Pyramid at Giza

The Great Pyramid at Giza or the Giza Necropolis is in the southwest area of Cairo. It has become the most famous Egyptian temple. It took three generations for the pyramid to be finished. It was started by Khufu, and Khafre and Menkaure added their input during 2500 BC. This pyramid is considered the oldest and the only remnant of the Seven Wonders of the Ancient World to still exist. Archaeologists know more than 2 million stone blocks were used to build the temple over 20 years. The pyramid is 455 feet tall, making it the tallest pyramid in Egypt. This pyramid is also known as The Great Pyramid of Khufu or The Great Pyramid of Cheops. It contains three burial chambers. The first chamber is underground, and the second is above ground and considered the queen's chamber. The third chamber was for the King, which had a red granite sarcophagus in the center of the pyramid, housing his mummified corpse.

Khufu was the son of Snefru.

Great Sphinx at Giza

The Great Sphinx might be the only one mentioned in many books, but it is hardly the only one in Egypt. Its sheer size and location on the Giza Plateau are responsible for its notoriety above the avenue of sphinxes that existed at the Luxor Temple. The Great Sphinx is definitely one of the oldest and largest monuments of Egypt and of the world. Construction began in 2500 BC under the rule of Pharaoh Khafre. The Sphinx has the head of a human, but a lion's body. It is also mentioned in the story of Oedipus Rex. The statue is 241 feet long and 66.34 feet tall.

The Valley of the Kings

The Valley of the Kings is considered the royal necropolis located near Luxor and Thebes. During the New Kingdom, from 1539 to 1075 BC, the Valley of the Kings was used as a royal burial ground for important Pharaohs, Queens, and high priests. There were also several elites, who were wealthy people, buried in the tombs here. It is the burial location for Ramesses II, Seti I, and Tutankhamun. The tombs are the best representation that we have of religious and burial beliefs of ancient Egyptians. In these hallowed halls, mummification was performed preparing the wealthy elitists for the afterlife. For approximately 500 years the tombs were constructed in the Valley of the Kings. The area has 63 tombs and chambers, which all range in size from a simple pit to a tomb with more than 120 chambers. These chambers were decorated with Egyptian mythological symbolism. The downside of the great tombs was the pillaging early discoverers conducted, robbing the tombs of amazing artefacts. King Tut's tomb was the only tomb that did not see the extreme damage by these early looters.

The Temple of Hatshepsut

Hatshepsut, a female ruler of Egypt, was in charge from 1479 until her death in 1458 BC. The Temple of Hatshepsut was erected as a mortuary temple in honor of her. It is located on the west bank of the Nile below the cliffs at Deir el Bahari. This temple is a colonnade structure designed by Senemut. Senemut was a royal architect during Hatshepsut's rule. The temple existed for posthumous worship and to honor Amun. Using the cliffs, the structure was built in three layered terraces. It reaches a total of 97 feet in height. There are two long ramps, which reach the first and second levels. This area around the ramps was once a garden space, long gone due to the changes in nature over the years.

The Luxor Temple

Thebes was established as a city on the east bank of the Nile River. The city was founded in approximately 3200 BC. During this time, it was more of a trading post than a grand location. However, it started to expand during the Middle Kingdom, particularly when the Karnak Temple complex was established. A statue of Nysuerre, a Pharaoh of the 5th dynasty, was constructed in the city and another statue was added during the 12th dynasty to represent Pharaoh Senursret. Thebes was ruled by people said to be descendants of the Prince of Thebes. Other rulers included Mentuhotep II and

Amenemhat I. In Thebes the god Amun was worshiped, with a temple dedicated to this god.

In 1400 BC the Luxor Temple was built in Thebes. This time period is considered to be part of the New Kingdom. The temple was built to worship Amun, Chons, and Mut. All three were very important gods of the time. The temple was placed at the center of the Opet Festival, where the statues of the gods were escorted into the Luxor Temple, along an avenue of sphinxes, which connected an earlier Amun temple and the Luxor Temple.

The Abu Simbel Temples

Located in Nubia and under the Aswan Governorate rule of Egypt sit two temples built circa 1264 BC. Ramesses II requested these great temples be built as a monument to him and his queen Nefertari. He wanted to commemorate his victory during the Battle of Kadesh. The temples sit above the Aswan High Dam today, but they were originally in the path of Lake Nasser. A huge relocation process was undergone to preserve the temples, but also to create the Lake. The temples are built of rock, having been carved from the mountainside. The relocation process occurred in the 1960s, so visitors can still see the great temples on a visit to the area.

Karnak

Karnak is another New Kingdom creation from circa 1570 to 1100 BC. Karnak is a religious site and the largest ancient site of its type in the entire world. Several generations of Egyptian builders worked on the site to create the three main temples of Karnak. There are also smaller temples and outer temples that make up the site, which is 2.5 kilometers north of Luxor. The most famous area of Karnak is the Hypostyle Hall. The hall is 50,000 square feet, with 134 columns in 16 rows.

The Temple of Ramesses III

Medinet Habu is considered the temple of Ramesses III. It was built after Hatshepsut and Tutmosis III built temples in the same area. Ramesses III wanted his mortuary temple to be the largest structure in the area, and made sure it included workshops, storehouses and residences. The temple is dedicated to Amun, like the other two in the area. The temple became an administrative location for Western Thebes, and included a fortified wall and gateway to ensure it was safe from any military action from the Syrians. Ramesses III was a military man, which is probably why he wanted his royal palace and mortuary to be fortified. Today, a lot of the structure has not withstood the test of time- at least in the outbuildings and along all sides of the wall. There was once a harbor entrance that connected a canal with the Nile, but the desert covered this long ago. Medinet Habu was extended for several centuries by the Romans and Greeks. During the 1st through the 9th centuries AD the area was expanded and the temple was used as a Christian church.

Colossi of Memnon

During 1350 BC, the Colossi of Memnon were erected. They are two stone statues, both representing Pharaoh Amenhotep III. These colossi are meant to guard Amenhotep's mortuary temple. They were worshipped before and after his death. The temples and Amenhotep's resting place were largely destroyed by time; however, the statues remain, highly damaged and nearly featureless, but nevertheless still standing.

The Temple of Seti I

The Pharaoh Seti I is honored at the Temple of Seti I. It is a mortuary temple located at Abydos, on the west bank of the River Nile. The construction of this temple was started just before Seti I's death sometime around 1279 BC. Ramesses the Great, Seti's son, took over the construction of the temple. One of the most interesting facts about this temple is the King List. It shows a chronological list of most Pharaohs starting with Menes and up to Ramesses I.

The Temple of Isis

The Temple of Isis most often refers to the temple started by Ptolemy II and finished by the Roman emperors of the 300s BC. The temple was built to honor the goddess Isis, who was the wife of Osiris and the mother of Horus. The three gods/goddesses dominated Egyptian religion, which may be why Ptolemy II felt it necessary to erect a temple in Isis' honor. The legend says Osiris was murdered by his brother Seth, but Isis collected all dismembered body parts of Osiris and used her magic to bring him back to life. It was then that they conceived Horus. The temple represents the giver of life and is also associated with funeral rites, since she brought Osiris back to life. The temple is near the Aswan Dam, located on an island to save it from the 1960s Lake Nasser project.

The Temple of Kom Ombo

Kom Ombo was built under the direction of Ptolemy VI in the second century BC. There are two temples with symmetrical creation, so the main axis looks duplicated. There are two entrances, two colonnades, two courts and two hypostyle halls. There are also two sanctuaries. The temple has views of the Nile, since it sits on a high dune.

Temple of Edfu

The Temple of Edfu is a place to worship Horus. It is considered the second largest temple, smaller only than Karnak. It is also one of the temples most preserved today. Construction of this temple was also started by Ptolemy III, but was not completed until 57 BC by Ptolemy XII, who was the father of Cleopatra. Many elements of the New Kingdom temples are found within the Temple of Edfu, as well as some Greek elements like the Mammisi or house of birth.

Mastaba Tombs

Prior to the pyramids discussed in this section, the Egyptians had Mastaba Tombs. These tombs were often underground chambers for courtiers and Pharaohs. Mastabas were flat surface structures, with openings on at least two walls. The top brick, with the flat roof, was only meant to cover the opening underground where one would follow stairs to reach the actual burial chambers. Typically, these structures were rectangular in shape with sloping sides.

Check out the rest of the book on Amazon from one of the below links:

Amazon US: https://www.amazon.com/dp/B01ED10GOQ

Amazon UK: https://www.amazon.co.uk/dp/B01ED10GOQ

Made in the USA
Las Vegas, NV
10 January 2024

84162539R00046